CAT FACT FRENZY!

by Nikki Potts

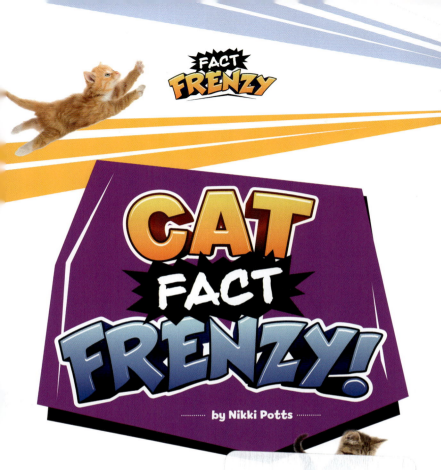

CAPSTONE PRESS
a capstone imprint

Published by Capstone Press, an imprint of Capstone
1710 Roe Crest Drive, North Mankato, Minnesota 56003
capstonepub.com

Cat Fact Frenzy! was originally published as *Totally Amazing Facts About Cats*, copyright 2019 by Capstone Press.

Copyright © 2026 by Capstone. All rights reserved. No part of this publication may be reproduced in whole or in part, or stored in a retrieval system, or transmitted in any form or by any means, electronic, mechanical, photocopying, recording, or otherwise, without written permission of the publisher.

Library of Congress Cataloging-in-Publication Data

Names: Potts, Nikki, author.
Title: Cat fact frenzy! / by Nikki Potts.
Other titles: Totally amazing facts about cats.
Description: North Mankato, Minnesota : Capstone Press, [2026] | Series: Fact frenzy | Audience term: Preteens | Audience: Ages 8–11 | Audience: Grades 4-6 | Summary: "Brace yourself for a CAT FACT FRENZY! Did you know that some cats can reach speeds of 35 miles per hour? Or that cats can make more than 100 sounds? Dozens of bite-size cat facts are paired with fun feline photos, welcoming in even the most reluctant readers. Whether kids are in the mood to browse or to devour a book from cover to cover, even a dedicated cat fan is sure to learn something surprising as they flip through these pages."— Provided by publisher.
Identifiers: LCCN 2024049161 (print) | LCCN 2024049162 (ebook) | ISBN 9798875233364 (hardcover) | ISBN 9798875233319 (paperback) | ISBN 9798875233326 (pdf) | ISBN 9798875233333 (epub) | ISBN 9798875233340 (kindle edition)
Subjects: LCSH: Cats—Juvenile literature.
Classification: LCC QL737.C23 P685 2026 (print) | LCC QL737.C23 (ebook) | DDC 599.75—dc23/eng/20241226
LC record available at https://lccn.loc.gov/2024049161
LC ebook record available at https://lccn.loc.gov/2024049162

Editorial Credits
Editors: Alison Deering and Ericka Smith; Designers: Jaime Willems and Tracy Davies; Media Researcher: Svetlana Zhurkin; Production Specialist: Whitney Schaefer

Image Credits
Capstone: Jon Hughes, 6; Getty Images: Fajrul Islam, 51 (middle), GlobalP, 14 (top), jonnysek, 48, Tuul & Bruno Morandi, 59; Shutterstock: 8th.creator, 24, Africa Studio, back cover, 3, 4, Aleksey Mnogosmyslov, 21, all_about_people, 23 (top), Alones, cover (bottom right), 23 (middle), Andy Dean Photography, 55 (back), Anurak Pongpatimet, 33 (bottom), Ares Jonekson, 35, ArtemPaimullin, 19, Aynur_sib, 22, Bilanol, 41, CkyBe (speech bubbles), cover and throughout, Constance Mannes, 50, Daria Bystritskaia, 57 (cat), david jonathan abasto, 28, DihandraPinheiro, 38, Ekaterina Kolomeets, cover (bottom middle), 33 (top), Elisa Putti, 26, Eric Isselee, 5 (bottom), 8 (left), 14 (bottom), 30 (middle), 49, Featureflash Photo Agency, 61, gn8 (rays and lines), cover and throughout, Happy monkey, 5 (top), Impixmart (cat silhouettes), 7 (bottom) and throughout, Irina Vasilevskaia, cover (bottom left), 55 (front), 64, Iryna Kuznetsova, 12, 27, J_poso, 16, Jaguar PS, 60, KDdesign_photo_video, 5 (middle), LadadikArt, cover (cape), LedyX, 40, Lunochka, 10, M-Production, 39 (middle), majivecka, 51 (bottom), Margarett24, 36, Mary Swift, 62 (top), matrioshka, 11, Mia Huebscher, 58, Miramiska, 15, MirasWonderland, 7 (middle), Natalia Bachkova, 37 (top), NeMaria, 62 (middle), New Africa, 57 (turkey and table), Nils Jacobi, 52, Nynke van Holten, 39 (top), 43, Olga 777, cover (top right), Pefkos, 44, Polina Tomtosova (cat-themed background), cover, back cover, QBR, 9, Rasulov, 13, RJ22, 34, s8, 42, Saley Yanny, 17, Seregraff, 20, Sergio Photone, 29, sophiecat, 31, 47 (left), 63, Stu Porter, 53, Studio-N, 56, studiomiracle, 45, TarasBeletskiy, 25, Tony Campbell, 1 (bottom), 8 (middle right), v_kulieva (gradient background), back cover and throughout, Vikafoto33, 30 (top), Vivienstock, 46, VixonPhoto, 54, Wilm Ihlenfeld, 37 (bottom), yevgeniy11, cover (top left), 1 (top), 8 (top right), Yuliia Sonsedska, 18, 32, Zerbor, 47 (right)

Any additional websites and resources referenced in this book are not maintained, authorized, or sponsored by Capstone. All product and company names are trademarks™ or registered® trademarks of their respective holders.

Printed and bound in the USA. PO 6307

TABLE OF CONTENTS

A Not-So-Small Collection of Cat Facts.......**4**

Ancient Cat Facts **6**

Basic Cat Facts **12**

Superlative Cat Facts **46**

Famous Cat (and Cat Owner) Facts......... **56**

A NOT-SO-SMALL COLLECTION OF CAT FACTS

Love cats? Great! Want to know ABSOLUTELY EVERYTHING there is to know about them? (Of course you do.) Well, we can get you started. For example, do you know what Australians think about black cats? (You do? Well, maybe skip page 15.) What about the Egyptian word for cat? If you're eager to find out these facts and much more, brace yourself and turn the page for a frenzy of cat facts!

ANCIENT CAT FACTS

Wild cats date back to prehistoric times.

WOW!

THERE ARE MORE THAN 35 BREEDS OF WILD CATS.

Domesticated cats have been around for about 8,000 years.

One legend says cats were created when a lion on Noah's Ark sneezed and two kittens came out!

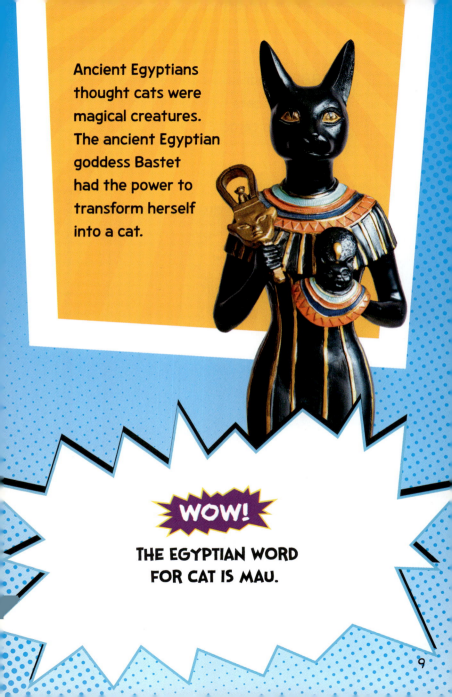

Ancient Egyptians thought cats were magical creatures. The ancient Egyptian goddess Bastet had the power to transform herself into a cat.

WOW!

THE EGYPTIAN WORD FOR CAT IS MAU.

In 1888, hundreds of thousands of mummified cats were discovered in an Egyptian cemetery.

Ancient Egyptians would mourn the death of a family cat by shaving off their eyebrows.

BASIC CAT FACTS

A female cat is called a queen or a molly.

A male cat is called a tom.

KITTY IS ONE OF THE TOP CAT NAMES.

Albino cats are rare. They are born without any pigmentation, or coloring.

Most cats have stripes, spots, or rosettes.

WOW!

IN THE UNITED STATES, SOME PEOPLE CONSIDER BLACK CATS BAD LUCK.

WOW!

IN AUSTRALIA, BLACK CATS ARE THOUGHT TO BRING *GOOD* LUCK.

Cats have around 230 bones.

WOW!

ADULT HUMANS HAVE JUST 206 BONES.

Adult cats have 30 teeth.

Cats can't see directly in front of or below their noses.

A cat's eye has three eyelids.

A cat's ear is controlled by 33 different muscles.

Cats can move their ears 180 degrees and separately.

Cats can hear sounds up to about 64 kilohertz.

WOW!

HUMANS CAN ONLY HEAR UP TO ABOUT 20 KHZ.

A CAT CAN RECOGNIZE ITS OWNER'S VOICE. (BUT IT OFTEN CHOOSES TO IGNORE IT!)

Cats can make more than 100 sounds.

Most adult cats only meow to communicate with humans.

The bumps on a cat's nose are unique to each cat.

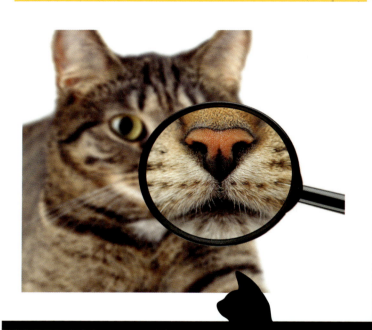

Whiskers help cats determine if they can fit into a space.

A cat's whiskers typically grow to be as long as the cat is wide.

FAT CAT = LONG WHISKERS!

Cats have an extra organ in the roof of their mouths that lets them "taste" the air. It is called the Jacobson's organ.

Unlike humans, cats can drink some salt water. Their kidneys filter out the salt.

You actually shouldn't give your cat milk. Most are lactose intolerant! They can't digest dairy products.

Cats can survive falls from high areas. Their bodies automatically twist around so they land on their feet.

Cats move their right feet first and then their left. Giraffes and camels are the only other animals to walk this way.

A cat can squeeze into small spaces because it has a free-floating clavicle—a bone that runs across its chest.

Cats have sweat glands in their paws. These glands also give off a scent that cats use to mark their territory.

Most male cats are left-pawed.

Most female cats are right-pawed.

All cats (with the exception of cheetahs!) can retract their claws.

Cats' claws all point back toward their limbs.

Because of the curl in its claws, a cat can't climb down a tree headfirst!

Cats sleep for about 70 percent of their lives. That's more than 16 hours of beauty rest per day!

A growth hormone is released when a kitten is sleeping.

Do your cat's whiskers and paws twitch while it's sleeping? If so, it's most likely dreaming!

Up to 50 percent of a cat's waking hours are spent cleaning itself.

Most cats don't like being in water. Wet fur can be heavy and cold.

But most Bengal cats love water.

WOW!

BENGALS ARE A MIX OF ASIAN LEOPARD CATS AND DOMESTIC CATS.

Female feral cats often stay in small groups.

Males are typically alone.

A group of cats is called a clowder.

A litter is a group of kittens born at the same time.

WOW!

LITTER IS ALSO THE WORD FOR WHAT DOMESTIC CATS PEE AND POOP IN.

All cats have natural hunting instincts.

Cats have played a part in the extinction of 63 different animal species.

SUPERLATIVE CAT FACTS

THE -ESTS OF ALL KINDS. THE BIGGEST, FASTEST, LONGEST, AND MOST TOES-EST.

The Egyptian mau is one of the oldest cat breeds.

The oldest cat lived to be 38 years and 3 days old. That's about 170 human years!

The rusty-spotted cat is the smallest wild cat. At just 1.8–3.5 pounds (.8–1.6 kilograms), it weighs about the same as a pineapple!

The world's longest domestic cat was a Maine Coon named Mymains Stewart Gilligan. He was 48.5 inches (123 centimeters) long.

A male Maine Coon can weight almost 20 pounds (9 kg). That's as much as a dining chair!

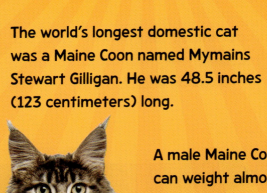

WOW!

THE MAINE COON IS THE OFFICIAL CAT OF THE STATE OF MAINE.

A cat named Jake holds the world record for the most toes. He has 28—seven on each foot!

WOW!

THE FAMOUS AUTHOR ERNEST HEMINGWAY HAD A POLYDACTYL CAT. THAT'S A CAT WITH EXTRA TOES!

A cat named Sophie Smith has the longest fur of any cat. Her fur is 10.11 inches (25.68 cm) long!

A domestic cat set a record speed of 30 miles (48.3 kilometers) per hour. That's faster than sprinter Usain Bolt!

Cheetahs are the fastest mammals. They can run more than 62 miles (100 km) per hour.

The most expensive breed of cats is the Ashera. It can cost up to $150,000 to purchase.

FAMOUS CAT (AND CAT OWNER) FACTS

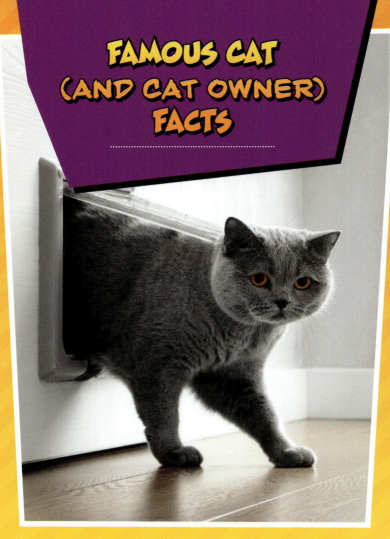

Some believe Sir Isaac Newton invented the cat door. It is believed he may have cut a door for a mama cat and, of course, a smaller door for her kittens.

President Abraham Lincoln was a cat lover and often brought home strays. Tabby and Dixie, two of his cats, often ate from the dinner table!

WOW!

OWNING A CAT LOWERS A PERSON'S RISK OF HAVING A STROKE OR HEART ATTACK.

WOW!

AN AILUROPHILE IS A CAT LOVER.

Disneyland has more than 200 cats.
The cats hunt mice in the park at night.

More than 100 cats live on an island in Japan. The human residents have created a cat shrine in the middle of the island.

Grumpy Cat went viral in 2012. Her frowny face made her an Internet hit. She has been the feature of many memes.

Stubbs the Cat was mayor of Talkeetna, Alaska, for 20 years. His office was located at Nagley's Store.

Lil Bub was a perma-kitten. She had kitten features for her entire life. Her lower jaw was shorter than her top jaw, and her teeth never grew in.

Felicette or "Astrocat" was the first cat in outer space. She was in space for 15 minutes before returning to Earth.

Maru is a Scottish straight cat that lives in Japan. His YouTube videos have been viewed more than 600 million times!

BOOKS IN THIS SERIES

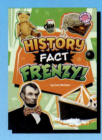